Hotel Fiesta

Hotel Fiesta

POEMS BY
LYNN EMANUEL

The University of Georgia Press
Athens

Library of Congress Cataloging in Publication Data

Emanuel, Lynn, 1949–
   Hotel Fiesta.

   I. Title.
PS3555.M34H6   1984   811'.54   84-2447
ISBN 0-8203-0728-9
ISBN 0-8203-0727-0 (pbk.)

FOR AKIBA, FOR DOROTHY

The publication of this book is supported by a grant from the National Endowment for the Arts, a federal agency.

Acknowledgments

The author and the publisher gratefully acknowledge the following publications where these poems first appeared:

American Poetry Review: "The Photograph of My Father at an Early Exhibit of Arshile Gorky," "The Last Two Photographs of My Father Before the War," "Grandmother Zoltana, Tunisia, Early '50s—Two Photographs—Before Her Death and at the Funeral," "Of Your Father's Indiscretions and the Train to California."
Extended Outlooks: The Iowa Review Collection of Contemporary Writing by Women: "The Sleeping," "She Is Six."
Georgia Review: "The Dig," "You Tell Me."
Poetry: "Frying Trout While Drunk," "The Photograph of Ramona Posing While Father Sketches Her in Charcoal," "When Father Decided He Did Not Love Her Anymore."
Prairie Schooner: "What I Know About the End of the Second World War," "The Artists."
Three Rivers Poetry Journal: "Elegy Written in the Vowels of Her Name," "Patient," "Discovering the Photograph of Lloyd, Earl, and Priscilla."
Slow Loris Reader: "Enormous Leisure."
Virginia Center for the Creative Arts Anthology: "Inventing Father in Las Vegas."
Anthology of Magazine Verse and Yearbook of American Poetry, 1984: "Of Your Father's Indiscretions and the Train to California" (reprint).

"Berlin Interior with Jews, 1939," "Of Father's Indiscretions and the Train to California," "The Sleeping," "Frying Trout While Drunk," and "She Is Six" are to appear in the *Morrow*

Anthology of Younger American Poets (New York: William Morrow, 1985).

I wish to thank The Virginia Center for the Creative Arts for a period of residence during which some of this book was written and the Pennsylvania Council on the Arts for a Creative Writing Fellowship.

Contents

I

black sedans,
long limousines

let dust remember, let dung remember
at the gate . . .

Frying Trout While Drunk

Mother is drinking to forget a man
Who could fill the woods with invitations:
Come with me he whispered and she went
In his Nash Rambler, its dash
Where her knees turned green
In the radium dials of the '50s.
When I drink it is always 1953,
Bacon wilting in the pan on Cook Street
And mother, wrist deep in red water,
Laying a trail from the sink
To a glass of gin and back.
She is a beautiful, unlucky woman
In love with a man of lechery so solid
You could build a table on it
And when you did the blues would come to visit.
I remember all of us awkwardly at dinner,
The dark slung across the porch,
And then mother's dress falling to the floor,
Buttons ticking like seeds spit on a plate.
When I drink I am too much like her—
The knife in one hand and in the other
The trout with a belly white as my wrist.
I have loved you all my life
She told him and it was true
In the same way that all her life
She drank, dedicated to the act itself,
She stood at this stove
And with the care of the very drunk
Handed him the plate.

The Sleeping

I have imagined all this:
In 1940 my parents were in love
And living in the loft on West 10th
Above Mark Rothko who painted cabbage roses
On their bedroom walls the night they got married.

I can guess why he did it.
My mother's hair was the color of yellow apples
And she wore a velvet hat with her pajamas.

I was not born yet. I was remote as starlight.
It is hard for me to imagine that
My parents made love in a roomful of roses
And I wasn't there.

But now I am. My mother is blushing.
This is the wonderful thing about art.
It can bring back the dead. It can wake the sleeping
As it might have late that night
When my father and mother made love above Rothko
Who lay in the dark thinking *Roses, Roses, Roses.*

Of Your Father's Indiscretions
and the Train to California

One summer he stole the jade buttons
Sewn like peas down Aunt Ora's dress
And you, who loved that trail of noise and darkness
Hauling itself across the horizon,
Moths spiraling in the big lamps,
Loved the oily couplings and the women's round hats
Haunting all the windows
And the way he held you on his knee like a ventriloquist
Discussing the lush push of grass against the tree's roots
Or a certain crookedness in the trunk.
Now everything is clearer.
Now when the train pulls away from the station
And the landscape begins to come around, distant and yet
    familiar,
That odd crease of yellow light
Or the woods' vague sweep framed in the window forever
Remind you of the year you were locked up at the Hotel Fiesta
While father went out with fast black minks.
And how wonderful it was
When he was narrow as a hat pin in this tux
And to have come all that way on his good looks.
How wonderful to have discovered lust
And know that one day you would be on its agenda
Like the woman who drank and walked naked through the
    house
In her black hat, the one you used to watch
Through a stammer in the drapes.
In that small town of cold hotels, you were the girl in the dress,
Red as a house burning down.

The Dig

He is filling the bucket with stones
And bringing the darkness up on a braided rope.
This will go on all day between the elm and iron gate.
The galvanized tin sings when it touches the rough balk
And the winch listens and the rope grows warm.
All day he has raised the dirt into this heaven of air.
I did not help. I poked my cup into the round
Eye of the bucket. I watched the shadows
Crawl inside and the wind limp stiffly
Through the little crooked places of tree and brandy.
All day he brings the darkness up until my heart
Is the bucket's round O of perpetual astonishment.
I put my hand across my eyes and listen
To the winch wind the rope around its shaft
And when I look a lizard is putting
Into my husband's hand her hands and her white
Stomach where one blue vein rides
From the groin to the throat.
I could have watched forever that slow work of muscle
In her neck, and something in the way he held her
Made me think of what we saw in ancient Eglon once:
A woman buried with her head in her lap, the cure
For infidelity, the old lust over-ended by the axe.
My husband worked all one night and in the end
I think he grew to love her, especially there,
With the earth on her like a black wing.

I Dream I Love You Under the Pine, Under the Poplar

I lie down
Always the same way

As though struck, anyway, I lie down
Again and again

Because I am young
And you are stroking me

Resinous branch, slowly, slowly,
A horse arises from that distant

Luxury of poplar—
Like silver breathed on—

The whole tree turns a bright
Haze in the wind.

It's you again, lacewing.
I live behind my eyes

At the eave and gable of myself
Thick with the larks

And the bells from whose lead throats
Cries topple, the unattainable

Brought close. From here I can see
Lilies and underneath the bulb

Like a sick extremity
Swollen, inert,

A vine vagrant along a limb.
I have read that on a bridge

In Nagasaki you can see
The shadow of a man still mounting

The shadow of a horse.

Berlin Interior with Jews, 1939

This is the year Europe looks up in sublime disregard
From the margin between two wars' classic accessories.
I am tired of the standard pictures of the Jews.
Even the Black Forest reminds me of my grandfather
Whose watch hands were tiny as pine needles.
I am tired of the fire twisting on the hearth where the maid
Brews hot mint tea in the middle of summer,
Tired of the sweet lip of the glass she lifts
To her mouth, tired of the reading of the *Aeneid*
And Dido lying down on the burning pyre—
Goodbye, goodbye the fire whispers to her flesh
Although no one listens. I am tired of my grandmother
Having to stand at the window to watch a train
That trickle of darkness at the horizon, slow, slightly crooked.
This is the year only the lamplight sleeps
Against her breast, the year she will wear her husband's
Gloves to bed because the buttons at the wrist,
Small, shiny as the eyes of her parakeet,
Stare as though they know her and this is the year
The maid in her red shawl bending to the kettle
On the hearth resembles a flame blown down by wind
And is about to be snuffed back to the wick of her black
   shoes.

When Father Decided
He Did Not Love Her Anymore

Tonight I will remember the model
With the wide, sad mouth
Who used to pose for father
Because I love the dangers of memory,
The boarded window and door,
Rooms where one bare bulb
Makes shadows swell up the wall.
And yet I recall only vaguely
The way her hem rustled on the floor
Like sand against tin
Laisse-moi tranquille, epicier,
It said because I want it to
Say something memorable.
I want her back
That brilliant, farfetched woman
Who drank coffee in our garden
And the days father fed me
Absinthe through a sugar cube
So I would be asleep by noon
And wake to find Ramona posing
Naked with a tambourine.
Tonight the whole world is a garden
In which the immortal whispers
Something about art
And its opportunities:
Memory like a bolt of silk
In a tailor's arms
Can be made into anything
Especially misfortune,
Especially the year Ramona spent

In a wrath almost Biblical
And so far from the world
Not even the moon could find
Her study in Paris
Where the doors opened to the river.

Grandmother Zoltana, Tunisia, Early '50s—Two Photographs—Before Her Death and at the Funeral

Even now it makes me thirsty to see her leaning in the
    doorway
Peeling peaches with her teeth.
Behind her rises the geometry of mosques and houses,
The ceaseless wheedling of a fountain—
These are the years of my voluptuous youth
And how cool it is when she washes
The soft stumble of broken stones leading to our house.
Somewhere inside I am watching the sweep of her hem
As she comes up from the beach and sits drinking beer
From a wet brown bottle and tells me goodbye
And goodbye whisper the cisterns of sweet water
Hidden under Carthage, goodbye the oars of the
    quinqueremes,
The harbor, and the way the fire whispers in her ears
As she stews four red peppers with wine and oil.
—This is the summer I grow afraid of the dark
Transforming itself into long sedans
Like those in the left-hand corner of the second photograph
Where boys are writing Arabic in the dusty windshields
And grandmother lies, attended by her priest.
In a long closet a man's silk tie lisps in my ear.
That night I undress in the gloom with grandfather watching
My hands nibble at their buttons and then
I am there: each nipple a boutonniere
Like the ones worn by men with thin black hair who carry
Grandmother and then me to bed.

Ordinary Objects

"Hic et ubique?"

HAMLET TO THE GHOST

I am letting them stand
For everything I love:

The light's unsteady scale
Across the glass, the hard

Brown grit of ants among the roses,
The bittersweet —

Everywhere I look I will see
Italy. The flowers will be full

Of prisons and churches,
Of women in black dresses, full

Of motorcycles and genuflecting.
The nightshade's dark, crooked stem

Is your street
And the water in the vase the sea's

Horizon tilting with the tilt
Of your ship. I am going to let

The daffodil be your mistress.
She is tired of you and stands

Looking at her feet.
In the fan's slow wind

The curtains reach for you.
I am full of grief. I am going

To lie down and die and be reborn
To come back as these roses

And wind myself thorn by
Thorn around your house

To fit into the nutshell
And the flat seed, the scar,

The door, the road, the web,
The moon's bald envious eye

Staring at you through the drapes.

Dream About the Old Mosaic
Found in a Syrian Orchard

I have come through
The sudden starlight of gunfire

To view on another fragment
Of tessellated floor

Another Dido.
Over the beehive ovens' imbricate roofs

Smoke is gathering, over the boy
Teasing hoops down tilted streets,

Over nighties in the wind.
They seem to want to come—

Through all the long luxury of shade
Between rug merchant and public bath—

Into the orchard with its blur of plums.
This is heaven, so cold my teeth ache,

Even midsummer when the sun is the color
Of shaved pine beneath a pot.

A woman is lying oddly marred on a pyre.
All that is left of the rest of the world is a hand.

In the dream I am a green hill with an eye.
Nothing, really, earth staring at fire.

The Photograph of My Father
at an Early Exhibit of Arshile Gorky

Here he is standing beside *Agony*—sad and proprietary—
While women in silk stockings whisper as they pass,
  mistaking him for Gorky.
They think he is there to admire himself, but I know
He is waiting for me, hands in his pockets because of the dirt
  under his nails. Beside him a lover smokes like a gun.
Suppose I were she and after this photograph was taken
We had gone out joyriding in the black sedans of the 1940s
Past the hotel where grandmother's teeth smiled at us from a
  glass of water,
Past the back porch of the Cook Street house in Denver
Where he used to wear his red kimono with Mt. Fuji rising
  from the mist,
Past Paris, past red Datsuns whizzing past Rue Baudelaire
And rooms filled with the chug chug of love, past all shores
Where the sea pours its cool threats and past and past
And past until the darkness carried us into the forest
Like two stones in its pocket—blind and still and immortal
As anything on earth.

The Photograph of Ramona Posing
While Father Sketches Her in Charcoal

Father is transforming Ramona
Into a streamline of flesh
Smudging the nipple with his thumb
In the tough, awkward way
Children rub their eyes when tired.
The sea is smooth as oiled stone again
Between Cagnes-sur-Mer and Cap Bénat
And the shadows full of models' empty shoes
Because this is 1938 and the tedium and heat
Of the Côte D'Azure.
Even Ramona is boring in the slick
Cool silver of her flesh.
Life is not pretty
Although she does not believe it.
This girl whose gold tooth
Father polished with his tongue
Could make anyone forget the wild buttocks of Rubens
And fill the fields with weeping painters
For whom the world has become a studio
Of beautiful forgeries.
Life is not pretty
Although they do not know it yet—
And in that heat
And the streets full of Germans.

Apology

Tonight I lie staring into the unlit neighborhood
And remembering Maria Bauder at whose windows
I threw stones from behind a trellis of dead roses.
She was German and that year school resurrected
The war in Europe until all night long trains
Of dead children flashed past like light
On a hypnotist's gold watch. It has been a long time
Since that evening when, full of sulk and swagger,
I leaned in my mother's dormer watching as Maria entered
From her bare yard to ours filled with the soft
Exaltations of light. From the branches of black
Walnut the great weight of the moon leaned out.
I overheard her accusations and then came down
Into the issuance of my name and stood on the porch
In the chilly updraft of self-pity and said I was sorry
Under a sky tall and decorated with stars as a general.

Self-Portrait

Tiresome, tiresome is the poet
Recumbent on the davenport
Lost in raptures of self-regard.
Give me poetry but pure
Before *charcuterie* and *bistro*
And distracted poses in tilted mirrors.
I am what is wrong with America.
Standing debauched, bereft,
Empty-handed for first one
Eternal verity and then another,
I am tired of all my yawn and barter.
How boring beauty is:
All chives and savannas,
The lush populations of grasses,
Are one vast atelier for the abstract.
Despite my lovely diction
I am going to die
Lying on an iron bed in stocking feet.
Oh no, oh no says the portrait
But so beautifully it is almost yes.

The Artists

. . . darkness is awake upon the dark.

D. H. LAWRENCE

I was not alive when you posed in silk trunks for Matisse
Or kissed Ruth Roman in front of the theater.
But I remember Mikonos:
The day we amazed ourselves, undressed, and walked
From noon into the wide syllables of water.
I saw your long eyes close.
I am in this picture:
White, masked, falling, here
Where everything is falling
As the clouds change their minds overhead.
It was warm, then cold—we fought the warnings and forgot
Everything except that conspiracy
Taking us league after untranslated league
Until gravity relinquished us.
And then the darkness settled, we had arrived
At the place where ships went down;
You hovered before me casting a long light onto the wreckage.
Father, something happened here: the craft had been
      rapturous
On water and the helmsmen, dozing, thinking their job done,
Woke to find dolphins in the masts.
I imagine these voyagers finally gave up,
Opened their lips,
And went as simply as you
Or I into that visitation.

Patient

I remember my mother on her hard knees
Complaining to the floor about the rich,
Her voice rough across the slick rise
Of their culpabilities, her hand moving
From the zinc bucket to the floor
Beside the bed in which I waited, sick,
For the cold kiss of salt and wet bread.
She fed me that lump on a tarnished spoon
While long limousines climbed the tipped hill
To the house where the man my mother loved
Shared the bright, empty plate of his table
With his wife. At night my mother would lie
Small and white as an egg in an apron, silent
As a snake laying its green throat on a pillow
Of stone. She thought about him until his face,
Like a moth wing worn away by the soft
Fascination of a child, crumbled to odds and ends
Under the tall black chill of common sense.

Of My Father Before the War

Suppose I were leaning in a doorway in Marseilles watching a
    volley
Of far clouds while two men quilted the water with their nets.
Suppose I were the one caught by the rain while the sea
    rinsed the docks
And gave the pilings a fat and oily slap
And suppose everywhere the cruise ships were setting off,
Violins swooning in the ballrooms, each liner lit up
Like Versailles. *Après moi le déluge,* I might say
As the great fleets of 1938 left me with the smoke
From my cigarette unraveling in my mustache.
And suppose one ship with a huge feather of steam above the
    stack
Let down its gangplank and I watched a woman in a veiled hat
Come hurrying forward. Father, this blur in the tripped
    shutter
Might be someone who could smuggle you out.
But what if I were grouped with all the houses in the cool
Silver of February and one garret were filled with the work
Of my blunt brushes. What if I had keys hidden in my pocket
And a lover lazily unzipping her dress when the woman who
    could save me
Waved and cried and disembarked into the vast nonchalance
    of France.

II

Miss Christina,
Miss Lorraine

Let the wild beasts and the sky's birds eat and remember.
Let all of them remember, so I can rest.
       YEHUDA AMICHAI

After Your Letter of Elegant Goodbye

This is a road where I could die for love
Nosing the car toward the black falls

The noise of an axe working
Its own way through woods that stand between me

And a view so suicidally inviting
A man has decided to build a house.

This is where I kill the lights,
Coast out toward the cutting of two-by-fours.

Beyond the skeletal bedroom, nothing but down:
The forest is fine and dry as loose handfuls

Pulled from a hen.
Even in this heat he has built a fire,

The mouth of a barrel crammed with burning lath
A blossom of sour smoke growing from charred strata.

I envy him the pines that lavish
His roof with soft touches, the bell of millet

He tied on a low branch swings silently
Above a town tipped with steeples.

I am so tired I could lie down among these trees
Until I was nothing

And let the earth take one slow liberty
After another.

You Tell Me

You tell me you're the stranger in bad weather,
I'm the girl hitching east in your dream.
You tell me I think it's beautiful:
The storm approaching on the solid body of wheat,
Clouds knotting the light
And each root connecting in the furrows
Until the acres tear under the thresher
As easily as old silk.
Which is not your freedom.
You have chosen to see how the sun is blank as a tack,
And we come past Leadville lonely, fighting,
On roads where people die each winter
Parked like lovers in their cars.
You try to explain about the workers,
Barges, coal, pipe, some small town
Where the dead have their churches and we stop
To watch a seizure of light in an open door.
I am slightly drunk, a young widow
With a tiny gun, riding out of Wichita
Toward Pittsburgh—all those broken homes,
The smell of sulphur and the fire
Where men exhaust themselves in shifts,
You tell me.

Desire

This is not Turner's Venice,
Not all the light is let loose across the canals,
The low clefts of little waves.
This is Pittsburgh where the air is sulphurous
And the water landlocked, slowed by waste and those small
    iron bridges.
But even here we have discovered desire, like Columbus
Who was looking for the end of the world and stumbled on
    continents.

In the elms there are supple constellations of light.
We are sitting in the yard and I, too, am hoping for the end
Of something, of the world, maybe,
That great still perfect lip and those little boats going off.

But it is August and this
The most familiar place in the world,
Calm water, boats, channels
And beautiful, too, those little bridges
Leading back and forth across the river.
Here in our own back yard we can find
The rare acres of stars, the thin wind
Abating in the huge green hesitations of the trees.

Tourists

In Tunis we try to discuss divorce
And dying but give up to lounge

With rug merchants under a plum tree.
From its corner the lamb's severed head

Watches the flies drink from its eyes
And its fat disappear into the fire.

The light rinses the edge of your sandal,
The two wasps that ornament the blur

Of screened window. My grandmother
Would have loved a night like this.

In the wind chimes I can hear her tea cart
With its china rolling through Cook Street's

Stony yard one summer when I was always
Thirsty, and she moved like a figure

On a clock from my lawn chair to the cart,
Or swabbed me with alcohol, or cut

My hair with the straight razor.
I was a week out of the hospital.

Beneath my breasts an incision was crossed
With stitches of surgical thread.

The scalpel came so close it gave
My heart a quick kiss. I nearly died.

Years later I can still see the skin
Flutter on the inside of my left breast

And my heart limps like a great uncle
Who, because he was a Jew and lame,

Was dragged by cossacks across the steppes.
He became a friend asking a favor

Of a horse who ran so hard, so perfectly
Hard, that the green grass rose to meet him.

She Is Six

She sleeps on a cot in the living room.
This is her father's mother's house.
And in the kitchen the men run their knife blades
Across the oilcloth with roses on the table
And grandmother cooks them steak and eggs.
She is pretending to be asleep but she is listening
To the men talking about their friends
And grandmother in her white dress
Walks back and forth past the door
And a hand reaches for salt and water.
Her father talks about divorce.
Now it is quiet.
Grandmother has left, her tight stockings
Showed rainbows,
And someone's upstairs undressing,
His dog tags making faint noise.
Her father walks into the room.
He is naked and there are certain
Parts of him that are shadows.
And he pulls the blankets to the floor
And then the sheet—as if not to wake her—
And he lifts her up and whispers his wife's name—
Rachel, Rachel
And he takes her hand, small with its clean nails,
And he puts it to the dark:
Oh Rae, Oh Rachel he says
And over his shoulder she can see
The long hall mirror framed in black wood
And she smells lavender in her father's hair

And then he gets up, first onto his hands
And knees like someone playing horse,
And puts her on the chair
And she sits and rocks like a deaf woman.

Discovering the Photograph
of Lloyd, Earl, and Priscilla

These are the great discoveries of my middle age:
This roadhouse in Omaha where Uncle Lloyd is nursing
Highballs with an ex-G.I. named Earl.
She's here, too, leaving a damp pink parenthesis
On the rim of her glass. The men are bored
But the girl whose name hisses like an iron across damp shirts
Peels open a pack of cigarettes and fills the room with smoke.
I have always wanted a coziness like theirs:
Rain touching the roof and someone trying to explain about
    Labor—
I might have been the waitress mopping up tips with a damp
    hand,
The one who loved Earl all those years while toting armloads
Of cobblers made from berries tiny as black caviar.
Tonight in an open window someone's stylus unzips a faint
    piano.
It must be 1947, Earl slicing salted melon from the rind,
Drinking the juice off his plate and the waitress going home
To count the dresser knobs until she falls asleep.
Tonight I find I envy the rain turning Omaha to
    daguerreotype,
Mud roads running amber as the veins in bad marble.
It is getting late. In the background beyond Earl and the
    waitress
There must be gardens. Roses, bowed down by their own
    heaviness,
Each day grow more perfect and more neighborly.
There must be graves and each separate grave is sending out
Its separate ghost.

Inventing Father in Las Vegas

If I could see nothing but the smoke
From the tip of his cigar, I would know everything
About the years before the war.
If his face were halved by shadow I would know
This was a street where an EATS sign trembled
And a Greek served coffee black as a dog's eye.
If I could see nothing but his wrist I would know
About the slot machine and I could reconstruct
The weak chin and ruin of his youth, the summer
My father was a gypsy with oiled hair sleeping
In a Murphy bed and practicing clairvoyance.
I could fill his vast Packard with showgirls
And keep him forever among the difficult buttons
Of the bodice, among the rustlings of their names,
Miss Christina, Miss Lorraine.
I could put his money in my pocket
And wearing memory's black fedora
With the condoms hidden in the hatband
The damp cigar between my teeth,
I could become the young man who always got sentimental
About London especially in Las Vegas with its single bridge—
So ridiculously tender—leaning across the river
To watch the starlight's soft explosions.
If I could trace the two veins that crossed
His temple, I would know what drove him
To this godforsaken place, I would keep him forever
Remote from war—like the come-hither tip of his lit cigar
Or the harvest moon, that gold planet, remote and pure
   American.

Elegy Written in the Vowels of Her Name

I have always loved Rogier Van Der Weyden's *Portrait of a
    Woman*
Because there is, between the little landscape of the hands—

Worldly like my grandmother's—and the impossible piety
In that face, a hidden commerce. It reminds me of the summer

My grandmother, brokenhearted, sat measuring a cool lapful
Of dried beans into a basin at her feet and how heavy

And gold as coiled rope those afternoons when the shadow
Of the pine came for its slow visits, dropping its dark

Shawls across her heart until I thought she would disappear.
Her body, stunned by stroke, dragged like a boat at anchor

Between the smell of scorched linen and the window,
Through which she could see yachts open the huge

Curve of reflected sky and sail away, bay by blue unvoyaged
    bay.

Enormous Leisure

I remember how you entered the water
Where the current murmurs to itself
Interrupted, now and then, by a flank of rock.
We lived in the mewsy streets around the theater
With names like "Hamlet," "Ophélie";
"Rue de l'Arbre Sec" led us out
Past the stiff gestures of shore pine
To the water and we would dip our oars and drift
Further to see the blunt-nosed pitch of the yacht
And the air was haunted with the smell
Of oiled steel and teak.

We were enamored of the dark,
The chipped green-blue of water,
Our vision jumbled as we pulled out,
Black masked, perched on the bow like two monkeys
And tumbled through the kelp whose fine hands
Parted to nothing
—The sudden huge blue pressure of the Atlantic
And your body, thick, whitish-green
Like shark or rare marble.
As we knew it would, the reef exploded
The fish running against us, the long leaps
And twists of kelp stoked by the current
And the absolute silence where we drifted and I saw you
    once—
Against the buckling window of the surface—
Scissoring your arms and legs
Like some distant felon running
From the enormous leisure of the light.

At the Magritte Exhibition

To a woman whose forehead is like a white veranda
You explain your apprenticeship with sorrow.
You and *Lola De Valence* are caught
Among museum goers, amid showers and the moths
Dragging their wet wings across the glass
To get a look at *La Vie Secrète*.
I imagine the damp reaches of Montauk
And the Hudson tarnished, cool and bitter
And beyond Manhattan, Malibu, surf lathering the rocks
Bad luck lying in her hammock, expectant.
I imagine you know America is laughing
And Belgium and France and you will go home
Brokenhearted to begin another canvas,
The roses, again, or Notre Dame. I believe
Magritte is shaking his head at your yellow taxi.
I believe the roses are wrong. All night
Their cool, insolent faces watch your house,
The roses putting their roots down onto the faces of the dead.

Looking for the Old Rosebud Cemetery

There is nowhere to go except this detour
And the motel whose lit name

Drips like a jeweled earring. In the lounge
A woman runs a bored finger along the keys

Of an upright and damps the pedal until the notes
Slow to one long blur of sound.

Nowhere to go, nothing for miles
Except this black coast

Of pine and the truckers hauling lumber up
And down the steep angulation of the divide

Or dozing on the washed out, raw shoulder
Of the highway, the radio tuned to a woman's

Low voice almost overcome by sorrow—
Two angels roam on that far shore.

Beautiful dead end. Where are you?
I stop to let things stand clear

In the headlights: a sparrow dipping its beak
Into a bright spatter of millet someone's thrown

And drive back blind to Denver.

What I Know About the End of
the Second World War

In L.A. someone is kissing Veronica Lake
And here, outside the window, the neon says *Hotel Clover.*
Trains haul copper all night through the quiet state
While grandmother lays out knives in the parlor.
Down the long hall, guests slowly rock across each other,
Their skirts and trousers on the chairs.
It is raining. My mother comes into the room
And I can hear the slight noise of buttons and see
Her hands on her breasts, the way they follow
One another. And now she is all light, all shadow
Waltzing slowly in the room, hands on her forehead,
The sign outside repeating *Clover, Clover, Clover.*

On Returning to Carthage
to Excavate an Ancient Sacrificial Site

For the first time I could remember
Grandmother's hair breaking in a fine

Shiver from the braid,
Her house at the top of the sloped avenue

Below which the world grew small.
The Bay of Tunis stared—huge blue eye—

Until I was nothing, until I was not I
But someone who could wash out the urn burials

Of children sacrificed under every green tree
To Baal. How heavy, hot and bright the work

Of the boats whose nets gathered the sea
Into pleated wakes and then let go.

The water broke against the sloped stones
While I opened the round throats of those jars

And like my grandmother cleaning a pumpkin
Spooned out that mixture. All day I sent the tongue

Of hose water digging and found
There was no end to the possibilities of childhood.

It could be a splash of mud on the inner hollow
Of a curved jug, a group of gold beads.

Over and over the whole bone of the inner ear
Turned up intact like a bud of honey locust

About to blossom in my hands.
It could be anything. Even that.

Kiss

In the cooking pot my aunt's long spoon pets the lamb's
Severed head, anoints with oil its one terrible eye
Until it weeps at the flowers on her dress.
Where there was body once, now there is iron and fire.
I am here to help. I am here to put my hand under
The lamb's chin and tip it back as though for a kiss.
I am here to help the lamb with the axe
That halves the skull as I have heard my aunt halve
Her husband's name at night. I/saac.
The body cannot die. In the hard push of meadow
Behind the empty house I have seen the lamb's body
Ride a spit of peeled plum under my uncle's hand.
I have seen the lamb lie down in the fire and rise
To its cleft hooves. Through the dark doorway
Of the cut neck I have watched the heart leak
Fire and flower a dry foam of ash.
The body cannot die. I can see this.
When the throat is tilted to let the smoke loose
The lamb's shadow crawls forward, licks, then swallows
The whole rough tongue of stones where I lie.
It is too quiet. I can feel the uneven knocking
Of my heart like someone tired hobbling across a yard
To the plum tree that makes one shadow want to lie down
With another. I want to die. Death is nothing.
It is fire looking for a place to start. It is a word
On the tip of the lamb's halved tongue, a kiss strong enough
To carry the green wood into the meadow.

for Michael Harari

The Poet in the Garret in America

I come up here to be disembodied and abstract,
To feel the sycamore astir against my naked psyche.
All over the hill a swarm of windows lights up
As I sit watching the half-dead plum, one frail
Output of flower, one blossomy upfloat.
Mopery is my métier. I want to see something
Beyond this woman sleeping through the groan
Of airbrake and dead pine when truckers bear down
On Mount Sopris. By day she's a waitress
With a huge red hankie pinned above her heart;
By night she turns into poetry so magnificent
She leaves the whole world looking loutish
And obscure. America, I want to transcend you.
Like this cardinal in the sycamore I love
My own beautiful sensibility and have come here
To be issued an invitation as exact and stunning
As Eve's was in her green, frail and sacramental
World. Under all my winsome diction, you and I
Are standing toe to toe, the diurnal, the divine.
America, I am still hopeful and a woman of my time.

Other Titles in the Contemporary Poetry Series